Maths Vocabulary CHALLENGE

at Key Stage 1

William Hartley

Tarquin Publications

William Hartley is the author of some forty primary maths and science resource books. He has over 20 years teaching experience in both primary and secondary classrooms but now spend his time working as an educational consultant, freelance writer of books and inter-active online material. He also works as an occasional supply teacher. For relaxation he enjoys ornithology, motor sport and working as a volunteer countryside ranger.

Bullet Points for Teachers or Parents

- A simple way to find out if a particular worksheet is suitable for a particular class or child is to look at the answers on pages 41 & 42.

- The Vocabulary Check List on page 4 shows which words have been included in the worksheets and also lists a selection of other words which should be known by the end of Key Stage 1.

- The worksheets are a valuable resource for homework assignments and it is worth considering also giving each child a photocopy of the Vocabulary Check List on page 4.

- To encourage the renewed interest in accurate spelling, sixteen spelling tests using the KS1 words are given on page 44. Others can easily be constructed.

- Inside the back cover there is a statement of the structure of the National Curriculum for Mathematics and the place of this book within it.

- Encourage the use of dictionaries, encyclopedias and other reference material so that the meanings of unfamiliar words can be looked up immediately.

- Use the photocopiable individual record sheet on page 43 to record which worksheets each child has done and the scores obtained.

© 2000: William Hartley
I.S.B.N: 1 899618 42 2
Design: William Hartley
Cover: Magdalen Bear
Printing: Five Castles Press, Ipswich

Tarquin Publications
Stradbroke
Diss
Norfolk IP21 5JP
England

Contents

Mathematics Vocabulary Checklist for Key Stage 1

Included in Worksheets 1 - 16: Number and Handling data

add, addition, after, altogether, answer, array, before, between, bought, buy, calculate, change, cheap, cheaper, coin, column, compare, continue, correct, cost, count, dear, difference, digit, divide, divided, double, eight hundred, eighty, eighty-nine, eighty-two, eleventh, enough, equals, estimate, even, exact, exchange, fifteen, fifth, fifty, fifty-nine, fifty-three, first, five, forty-two, four, fourteen, fourth, fraction, graph, group, guess, half, halve, hundred, into, label, last, least, less, list, make, minus, more, most, multiplied, multiply, nearly, next, nine, nineteen, ninety, ninety-five, ninth, no, odd, once, pair, pay, pence, penny, pictogram, plus, pound, predict, price, quarter, right, roughly, round, row, score, second, sell, set, seven, seventeen, seventh, seventy-seven, share, six, sixteen, sixth, sixty-eight, sixty-three, sold, spend, subtract, sum, symbol, table, tally, tenth, thin, third, thirteen, thirty-eight, thirty-six, thousand, three, three-quarters, times, title, to, total, twenty-one, twice, two, vote, whole, wrong..

Additional recommended words
calculation, exactly, five hundred, forty, four hundred, jotting, left over, lots of, money, multiple of, nine hundred, none, number, operation, order, part, pattern, place value, puzzle, represent, rule, sequence, seven hundred, sign, six hundred, sixty, size, sort, take away, thirty, three hundred, three-digit, two hundred, two-digit, units.

Included in Worksheets 17 -36: Shape, space and measures

about, above, across, afternoon, always, analogue, anti-clockwise, apart, April, August, autumn, back, backwards, balance, bedtime, behind, below, bend, beside, birthday, bottom, capacity, centimetre, centre, circle, clock, clockwise, close, compare, cone, container, contains, cube, cuboid, curved, cylinder, December, deep, depth, digital, drawing, early, edge, empty, end, evening, far, February, flat, fold, fortnight, forwards, Friday, front, full, further, gram, hands, heavy, height, hexagon, high, higher, hold, holiday, hollow, hour, in, inside, January, journey, July, June, kilogram, late, length, light, lighter, lightest, litre, long, low, lower, March, May, metre, middle, midnight, millilitre, minute, Monday, money, month, morning, narrow, near, never, new, newest, night, November, now, octagon, October, often, older, oldest, on, one, opposite, outside, over, pentagon, point, position, pyramid, quick, quickest, rectangle, reflection, round, route, ruler, Saturday, scales, second, September, shallow, shape, short, shorter, side, sideways, size, slide, slow, slower, slowest, solid, sometimes, soon, sphere, spring, square, star, straight, summer, tallest, thick, three, through, Thursday, time, today, tomorrow, top, towards, triangle, triangular, under, up, watch, week, weekend, weight, wide, width, winter, year, yes

Additional recommended words
along, around, away from, circular, close to, corner, day, dinnertime, direction, down, face, half full, half litre, half past, half turn, in front, just over, just under, match, measure, mirror line, next to, o'clock, playtime, quarter past, quarter to, quarter turn, quickly, rectangular, right angle, roll, slowly, Sunday, surface, symmetrical, tape measure, thin, too few, too little, too many, too much, Tuesday, underneath, Wednesday, whole turn, yesterday.

Name ....

Class .... Date ....

Mark

1

Out of

12

TAKE YOUR PICK 1

Write the words in the correct column on the chart.
Circle or cross out each word once you have used it.

four	fifteen	seventeen	three
thirteen	seven	six	sixteen
five	nineteen	nine	fourteen

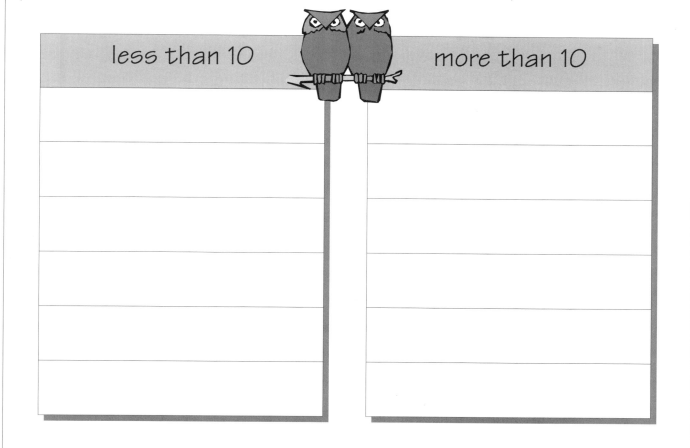

less than 10	more than 10

2	Mark	Out of 7

Name ....

Class ....   Date ....

ADDITION AND SUBTRACTION

Put each of these words in the correct sentence.

★★

double   difference   more   altogether

sum   make   equals

★★★

1. Twenty-six is _ _ _ _ than sixteen.

2. The _ _ _ of two numbers is the total you

   get when you add them together.

3. Five add nine _ _ _ _ _ _ fourteen.

4. When you _ _ _ _ _ _ a number you

   make it twice as big.

5. Four plus seven plus nine equals twenty

   _ _ _ _ _ _ _ _ _ _ .

6. A subtraction calculation finds the

   _ _ _ _ _ _ _ _ _ _ between two numbers.

7. Three and six and eight _ _ _ _ seventeen.

Name ....

Class ....   Date ....

CONNECT IT

Connect each number to its name.

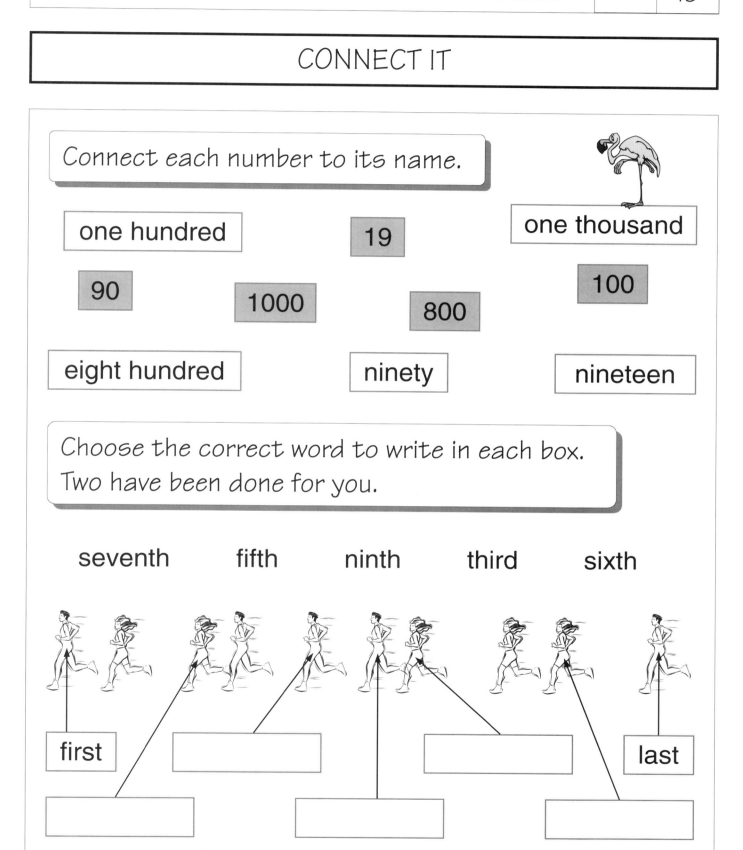

one hundred

19

one thousand

90

1000

800

100

eight hundred

ninety

nineteen

Choose the correct word to write in each box.
Two have been done for you.

seventh   fifth   ninth   third   sixth

first

last

4

Mark | Out of 8

Name ....

Class .... Date ....

MONEY WORDSEARCH

Write the missing letters in the words.

Find the words in the wordsearch.
Rule a line of a different colour over each one.

S	O	Y	P	D	E	P	E
E	B	H	E	N	I	O	C
L	D	X	N	Q	I	F	I
L	N	S	N	W	A	J	R
R	C	P	Y	B	U	Y	P
C	H	E	A	P	T	K	B
E	G	N	A	H	C	Z	U
G	S	D	L	V	M	C	A

P _ N _ Y

B _ Y

S _ L _

S P _ _ D

C H _ N G _

C _ E _ P

P _ I _ E

C _ I N

Name ....

Class ....   Date ....

SORT OUT THE WORDS 1

Read the clues on the left. Sort out the words in the middle and write them in their correct places in the column on the right.

Clue	Word	Correct order
1. Having no mistakes	once	1. _____
2. The one after the first	predict	2. _____
3. Incorrect	nearly	3. _____
4. Describe future events before they happen	correct	4. _____
5. Equal to 100p	fraction	5. _____
6. Almost	second	6. _____
7. A small part of something	pound	7. _____
8. At one time only	wrong	8. _____

6

Mark | Out of
10

Name ....

Class ....   Date ....

WORD GRIDS 1

Fit these words on the grid in their correct places.

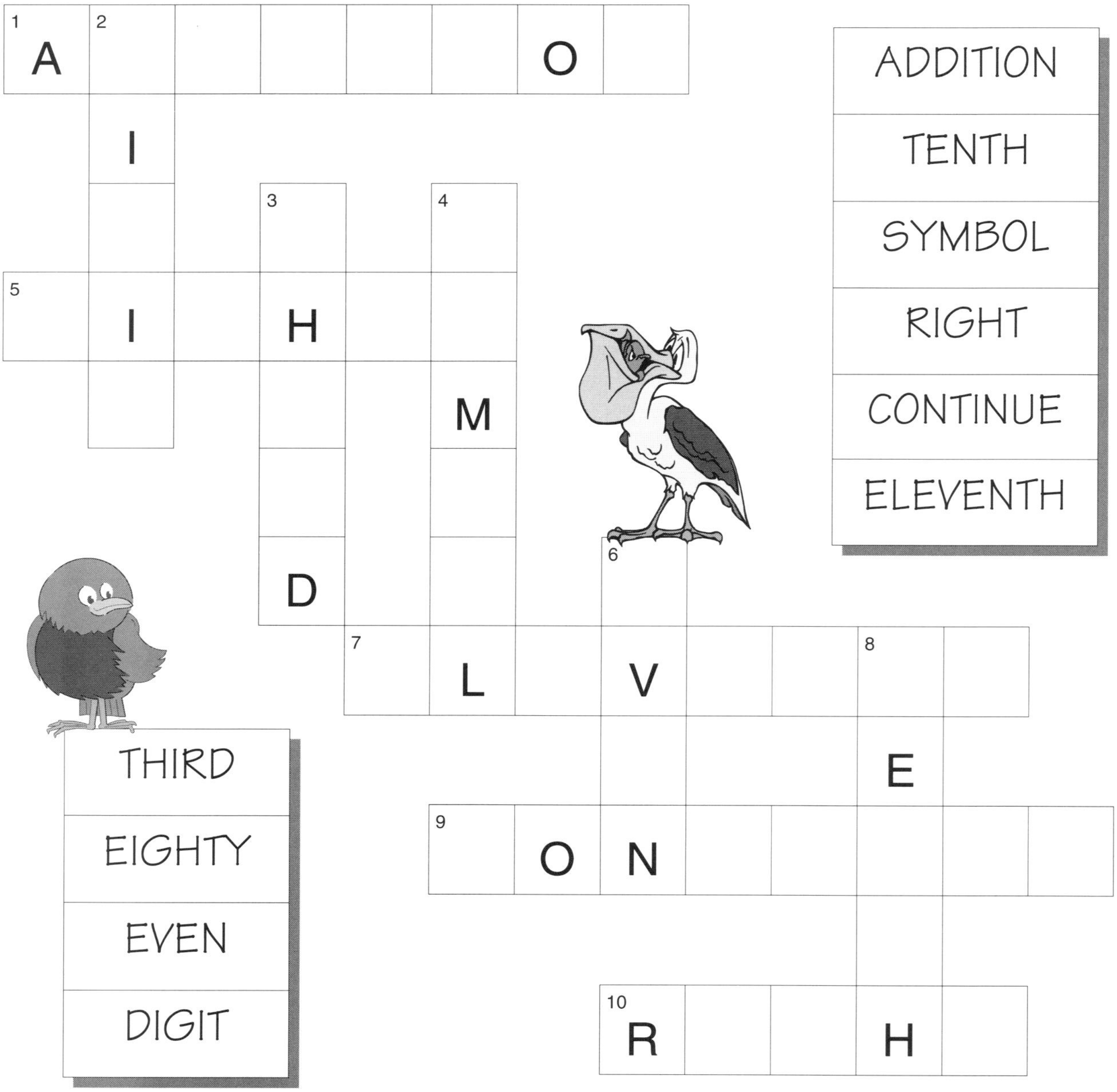

A   O

I

I   H

M

D

L   V

E

O   N

R   H

Word list (top box):
- ADDITION
- TENTH
- SYMBOL
- RIGHT
- CONTINUE
- ELEVENTH

Word list (bottom box):
- THIRD
- EIGHTY
- EVEN
- DIGIT

Name ....

Class .... Date ....

SHOPPING

Catch the floating words and put them in their correct places.

roughly

1. The shop _ _ _ _ many different types of things.

2. The pears and the apples were

   _ _ _ _ _ _ _ the same price. pence sold

3. The bananas were _ _ _ _ _ _ _ than the peaches.

4. The cost of the oranges was shown on the _ _ _ _ _.

5. Cabbages cost _ _ _ _ than lettuces.

less label Most pay

6. Many items had their prices marked in _ _ _ _ _.

7. You went to the check-out to _ _ _

   for the things you wanted.

8. _ _ _ _ customers paid in cash. cheaper

8

Mark | Out of | 8

Name ....
Class ....   Date ....

SOLVE IT 1

Read the clues on the left.
Arrange the mixed-up letters in the middle to make the correct word to put in the column on the right.

Clue	Letters	Correct word
1. In front of	forebe	1. b_____
2. Expensive	eadr	2. d_____
3. Coming before all others	tirsf	3. f_____
4. To estimate	uessg	4. g_____
5. Perfectly correct	actex	5. e_____
6. A number of things placed or classed together	oupgr	6. g_____
7. To swop one thing for another	chaexnge	7. e_____
8. An arrangement of things	ayarr	8. a_____

KS1 Maths Vocabulary CHALLENGE

Name ....

Class .... Date ....

CROSSWORD 1

Fill in the crossword.

¹A		²S		³E		■
	■		■		■	⁴O
⁵T			■		■	
	■	⁶R		U		
R	■		■		■	
■	■		⁷T			⁸N
⁹I			■			

ACROSS

1. The reply to a question

5. One add one

6. To bring a number to the nearest ten or unit

7. Thick and _ _ _ _

9. You go _ _ _ _ something when you go inside it

DOWN

1. Not before

2. The result in a game

3. As many as you need

4. The opposite of even

7. _ _ calculate means to work out something

8. The opposite of yes

10

Mark

Out of

12

Name ....

Class .... Date ....

TAKE YOUR PICK 2

Write the words in the correct column on the chart.
Circle or cross out each word once you have used it.

eighty-two	twenty-one	eighty-nine	sixty-three
thirty-eight	seventy-seven	fifty-three	fifty-nine
ninety-five	thirty-six	sixty-eight	forty-two

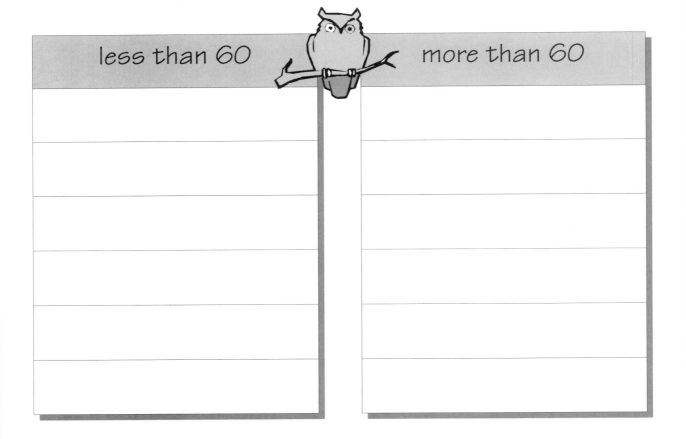

less than 60	more than 60

Name ....

Class ....   Date ....

MULTIPLICATION AND DIVISION

> Put each of the words at the bottom of the page in the correct sentence.

1. When you _ _ _ _ _ _ a number by four it becomes a quarter the size.

2. When you _ _ _ _ _ _ _ _ _ a number by two it becomes twice the size.

3. A _ _ _ _ _ _ of numbers is written down a page.

4. Sixty _ _ _ _ _ _ _ _ by ten equals six.

5. A _ _ _ of numbers is written across a page.

6. Ten _ _ _ _ _ _ _ _ _ _ _ by four equals forty.

7. To _ _ _ _ _ a number you divide it by two.

★★

| halve | multiplied | row | multiply |
| divide | column | divided | |

★★

12

Mark | Out of 12

Name ....

Class .... Date ....

FRACTIONS

What fraction of each shape is shaded?
Write your answer in the box.
Choose from the words given.

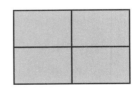

 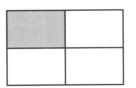 

whole	half	quarter	three-quarters

KS1 Maths Vocabulary CHALLENGE

Name ....

Class ....   Date ....

13

Mark   Out of
8

FOUR RULES WORDSEARCH

Write the missing letters in the words.

Find the words in the wordsearch.
Rule a line of a different colour over each one.

a _ d

d _ v _ d e

t _ m _ s

p _ u s

s h _ r _

m u _ t i _ l _

m _ n _ s

s _ b t _ a _ t

q	s	x	j	p	b	p	f
m	u	l	t	i	p	l	y
i	n	o	a	e	b	u	t
n	i	e	r	a	h	s	t
u	m	a	w	h	c	l	i
d	s	d	k	r	o	g	m
m	v	d	i	v	i	d	e
t	c	a	r	t	b	u	s

14

Mark | Out of
8

Name ....

Class .... Date ....

SORT OUT THE WORDS 2

Read the clues on the left. Sort out the words in the middle and write them in their correct places in the column on the right.

Clue	Word	Correct order
1. Two times	last	1. _____
2. The answer to an addition sum	fifty	2. _____
3. Two of the same kind	estimate	3. _____
4. The price of something	twice	4. _____
5. Coming at the end	fourth	5. _____
6. Quarter	pair	6. _____
7. Five times ten	cost	7. _____
8. To guess the size of something	total	8. _____

Name ....

Class ....   Date ....

WORD GRIDS 2

Fit these words on the grid in their correct places.

title

vote

table

least

bought

next

between

compare

tally

calculate

Grid clues:

1. (across) 2. l ... 3. t
4.
5. a ... y
s
e
6.
7. o ... e
8. e ... e
9.
x
10. u ... t

Name ....

Class ....   Date ....

DATA

Write each word in its correct place.
Be careful. This exercise is not easy.

list

count

set

graph

table

1. A _ _ _ is a group of things that belong together.

2. My friend asked me if I could _ _ _ _ _ up to fifty.

3. In a _ _ _ _ _ _ _ _ _ _ facts

are shown in picture form.

Tally

4. I made a _ _ _ _ of the things I needed from the shop.

5. A _ _ _ _ _ _ is one way of showing numbers

as a chart or diagram.

6. A _ _ _ _ _ is a list of facts or

pictogram

figures written in rows and columns.

7. _ _ _ _ _ marks can keep a record of a score.

Name ....

Class ....   Date ....

17

Mark | Out of
8

SOLVE IT 2

Read the clues on the left.
Arrange the mixed-up letters in the middle to make the correct word to put in the column on the right.

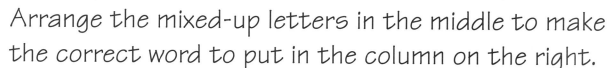

Clue	Letters	Correct word
1. The early part of the day	ningmor	1. m_____
2. A day off work or school	dayholi	2. h_____
3. The centre part of something	dlemid	3. m_____
4. A curve	ndbe	4. b_____
5. A twelfth part of a year	thmon	5. m_____
6. It tells the time	clcko	6. c_____
7. At the back of	hibend	7. b_____
8. A period of two weeks	nigfortht	8. f_____

18

Mark | Out of
| 10

Name ....

Class .... Date ....

CROSSWORD 2

Fill in the crossword.

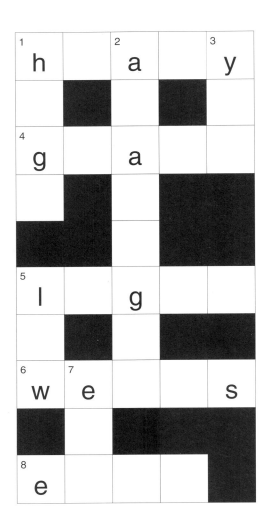

ACROSS

1. The opposite of light
4. Small units for measuring weight
5. Not weighing much
6. 52 of these in one year
8. The part along the side or end of something

DOWN

1. Going upwards for a long way
2. Type of watch or clock
3. The opposite of no
5. Not high
7. The place where something stops

Name ....

Class ....   Date ....

Mark **19**

Out of
12

2D or 3D?

Write the words in the correct column on the chart.
Circle or cross out each word once you have used it.

square	cube	cylinder	pentagon
star	circle	pyramid	sphere
cone	rectangle	cuboid	triangle

2D shapes	3D shapes

20

Mark | Out of **7**

Name ....

Class .... Date ....

MEASURING WORDS 1

Put each of these words in the correct sentence.

★★

width   narrow   compare   ruler

height   lighter   metre

★★

1. To _ _ _ _ _ _ _ lengths is to find out

   which is longest or shortest.

2. A pencil is _ _ _ _ _ _ _ in weight than a table.

3. One hundred centimetres is the

   same length as one _ _ _ _ _ .

4. The _ _ _ _ _ of an object is the

   distance from one side to the other.

5. A _ _ _ _ _ is a useful tool for measuring length.

6. A _ _ _ _ _ _ road is not very wide.

7. The measurement from the bottom to the

   top of something is its _ _ _ _ _ _ .

Name ....

Class ....   Date ....

21

Mark | Out of
7

MAKE IT MAKE SENSE 1

The words in capitals are in the wrong sentences. Sort them out and write the best word opposite the correct sentence number in the box.

1.	2.	3.

4.	5.	6.

7.

1. A circle has a SHORTER edge.

2. SLOWER I travel to school in a car.

3. A SOMETIMES is the sharp end of something.

4. A sprint race is won by the CURVED runner.

5. A centimetre is CONTAINS than a metre.

6. The POINT you travel the longer the journey takes.

7. My bag QUICKEST all the things I need for school.

22

Mark | Out of
8

Name ....

Class .... Date ....

MEASURES WORDSEARCH

> Write the missing letters in the words.

W _ I G H _

L E _ _ T H

H _ A _ Y

B _ L _ N C E

L _ G H _

K _ L _ G R _ M

S C _ L _ S

C E _ T I M _ T R _

> Find the words in the wordsearch.
> Rule a line of a different colour over each one.

S	M	A	R	G	O	L	I	K	T
E	Y	I	E	T	J	M	B	F	H
L	V	D	L	H	G	A	K	H	G
A	A	H	T	G	N	E	L	C	I
C	E	N	T	I	M	E	T	R	E
S	H	B	A	L	A	N	C	E	W

Name ....

Class ....   Date ....

23

Mark   Out of

8

SORT OUT THE WORDS 3

Read the clues on the left. Sort out the words in the middle and write them in their correct places in the column on the right.

Clue	Word	Correct order
1. The season before spring	year	1. _____
2. Beneath	winter	2. _____
3. Tells the time	spring	3. _____
4. The season after summer	watch	4. _____
5. The middle point of something	below	5. _____
6. The season before autumn	centre	6. _____
7. Twelve months	summer	7. _____
8. The season after winter	autumn	8. _____

24

Mark | Out of 10

Name ....

Class .... Date ....

WORD GRIDS 3

Fit these words on the grid in their correct places.

1 | 2 M | | | O | |

L

3

4 | E | | | E

SLOWEST

BEDTIME

TOMORROW

ACROSS

DIGITAL

NEWEST

5 | I | D

6

7 | A | | O | | 8

A

LATE

OLDER

HOLLOW

SIDE

9 | L | | T

10 | E | E

Name ....

Class .... Date ....

25

Mark | Out of
| 8

POSITION, DIRECTION AND MOVEMENT 1

Put the words on the signs in their correct places.

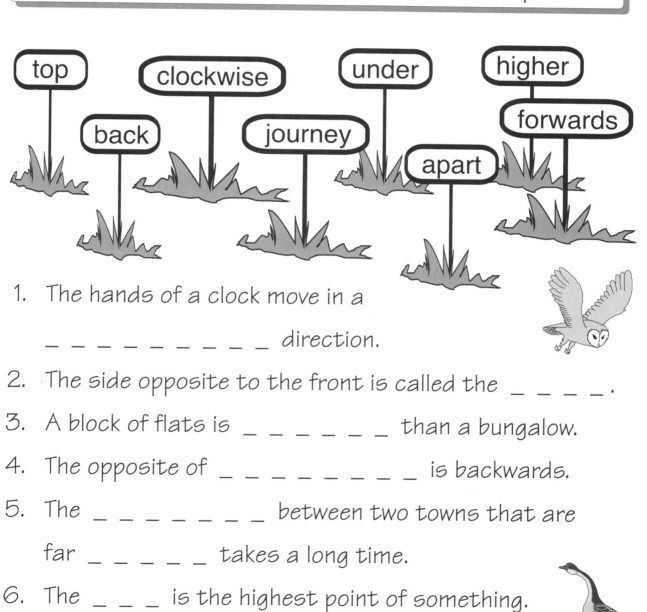

1. The hands of a clock move in a

   _ _ _ _ _ _ _ _ _ direction.

2. The side opposite to the front is called the _ _ _ _ .

3. A block of flats is _ _ _ _ _ _ than a bungalow.

4. The opposite of _ _ _ _ _ _ _ _ is backwards.

5. The _ _ _ _ _ _ _ between two towns that are

   far _ _ _ _ _ takes a long time.

6. The _ _ _ is the highest point of something.

7. The opposite of _ _ _ _ _ is over.

26

Mark | Out of

8

Name ....

Class ....   Date ....

SOLVE IT 3

Read the clues on the left.
Arrange the mixed-up letters in the middle to make
the correct word to put in the column on the right.

Clue	Letters	Correct word
1. The time when it is dark	htnig	1. n_____
2. At no time	reven	2. n_____
3. Not forwards or backwards but ....?	asdiewys	3. s_____
4. The place where something is	itposion	4. p_____
5. Fast	ickqu	5. q_____
6. 2D shape with eight sides	onagoct	6. o_____
7. Circle shaped	undro	7. r_____
8. The opposite of inside	ousidet	8. o_____

Name ....

Class ....   Date ....

CROSSWORD 3

Fill in the crossword.

¹L		²N			³W	
⁴T			⁵A		D	
E		⁶N				⁷O
	⁸I					
⁹O			¹⁰T			E

ACROSS

1. Not short

4. The dog came

   _ _ _ _ _ _ _ _ me

6. At the present time

9. The cat sat _ _ the

   mat

10. This is measured

    by a clock

DOWN

1. Unit for measuring

   capacity

2. Not already used

3. With sides far apart

5. More or less

7. Three minus two

8. On the inside of

28

Mark | Out of
12

Name ....

Class .... Date ....

MONTHS OF THE YEAR

Write the months of the year in order on the chart starting with January and ending with December. Circle or cross out each month once it has been used.

May	July	February	December
August	January	June	March
September	April	November	October

The months of the year

1.	7.
2.	8.
3.	9.
4.	10.
5.	11.
6.	12.

Name ....

Class ....   Date ....

29

Mark   Out of
              8

MEASURING WORDS 2

Put each of the words at the bottom of the page in the correct sentence.

1. The _ _ _ _ of something tells you how large or small it is.

2. The _ _ _ _ _ _ _ you are away from something the smaller it appears.

3. The opposite of near is _ _ _ .

4. Something that is _ _ _ _ _ is not far away.

5. The _ _ _ _ _ _ _ _ object among many is the one that weighs the least.

6. A _ _ _ _ _ _ _ container has little _ _ _ _ _ .

7. _ _ _ _ water can be dangerous

| further | close | depth | Deep |
| size | shallow | far | lightest |

30

Mark

Out of

8

Name ....

Class ....   Date ....

MAKE IT MAKE SENSE 2

The words in capitals are in the wrong sentences. Sort them out and write the best word opposite the correct sentence number in the box.

1. I do not go to school at the TRIANGULAR.

2. The day after Sunday is FRIDAY.

3. The picture you see in a mirror is called a TALLEST.

4. A REFLECTION shape has three sides.

5. I am the HANDS girl in my class.

6. Things that are far MONDAY are far away from each other.

7. The day before APART is Thursday.

8. The WEEKEND of a clock help you to tell the time.

1.	
2.	
3.	
4.	
5.	
6.	
7.	
8.	

Name ....

Class ....   Date ....

Mark   Out of
8

ASSORTED WORDS WORDSEARCH

Write the missing
letters in the words.

h _ l d

e m p _ _

f u l _

c _ p _ c i t _

a b _ v _

m _ l _ i l i _ r e

s l _ w

c _ n t a _ n _ r

Find the words in the wordsearch.
Rule a line of a different colour over each one.

e	r	e	n	i	a	t	n	o	c
m	c	l	h	k	e	i	b	w	h
p	k	e	v	o	b	a	j	o	o
t	f	l	a	j	g	f	u	l	l
y	t	i	c	a	p	a	c	s	d
m	i	l	l	i	l	i	t	r	e

32

Mark | Out of
8

Name ....

Class .... Date ....

SORT OUT THE WORDS 4

Read the clues on the left. Sort out the words in the middle and write them in their correct places in the column on the right.

Clue	Word	Correct order
1. A picture made with a pen or pencil	midnight	1. _____
2. The least new of the items	flat	2. _____
3. Day before Friday	oldest	3. _____
4. 2D shape with six sides	drawing	4. _____
5. 12 o'clock at night	minutes	5. _____
6. Thirty of these in half an hour	near	6. _____
7. Close to	hexagon	7. _____
8. Level and smooth	Thursday	8. _____

KS1 Maths Vocabulary CHALLENGE

Name ....

Class ....   Date ....

WORD GRIDS 4

Fit these words on the grid in their correct places.

deep

always

fold

beside

today

inside

opposite

birthday

through

evening

34

Mark

Out of

8

Name ....

Class .... Date ....

POSITION, DIRECTION AND MOVEMENT 2

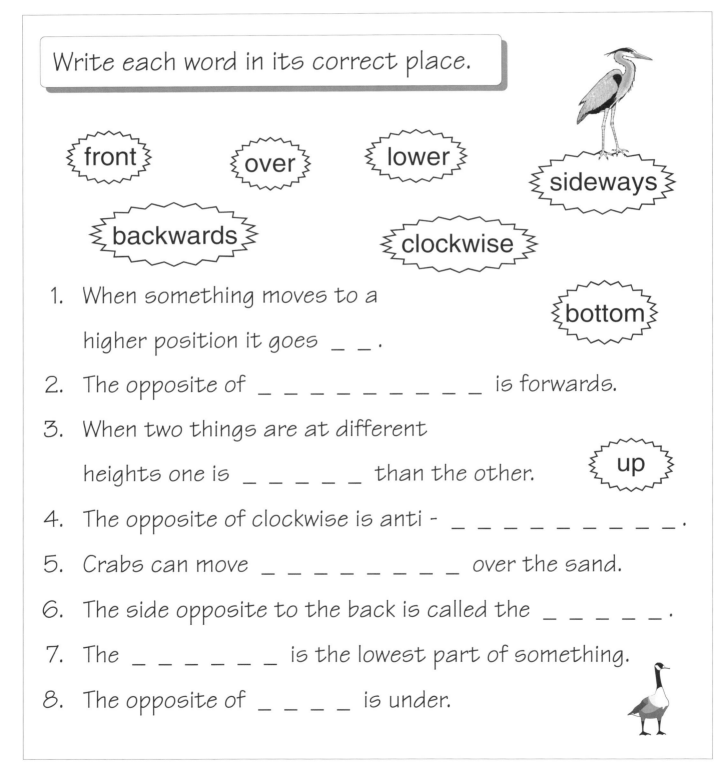

Write each word in its correct place.

front   *over*   *lower*   *sideways*

backwards   *clockwise*

bottom

1. When something moves to a

   higher position it goes _ _ .

2. The opposite of _ _ _ _ _ _ _ _ _ _ is forwards.

3. When two things are at different

   heights one is _ _ _ _ _ than the other.   *up*

4. The opposite of clockwise is anti - _ _ _ _ _ _ _ _ _ .

5. Crabs can move _ _ _ _ _ _ _ _ over the sand.

6. The side opposite to the back is called the _ _ _ _ _ .

7. The _ _ _ _ _ _ is the lowest part of something.

8. The opposite of _ _ _ _ is under.

Name ....

Class ....   Date ....

Mark

35

Out of

8

SOLVE IT 4

Read the clues on the left.
Arrange the mixed-up letters in the middle to make the correct word to put in the column on the right.

Clue	Letters	Correct word
1. In a short time	nsoo	1. s_____
2. To move smoothly over something	desli	2. s_____
3. The day after Friday	turSadya	3. S_____
4. Not liquid or gas	lidso	4. s_____
5. The way taken to get somewhere	outre	5. r_____
6. Comes between first and third	osecnd	6. s_____
7. The opposite of thin	ickht	7. t_____
8. Not bent	stghtrai	8. s_____

36

Mark | Out of
9

Name ....

Class .... Date ....

CROSSWORD 4

Fill in the crossword.

ACROSS

1. The outline of an object shows its _ _ _ _ _
3. Many times
4. Ten minus seven
6. A period of 60 minutes
7. You need this to buy things

DOWN

1. The opposite of long
2. The part of the day between morning and evening
5. Before the expected time
8. The duck swam _ _ the pond every day

Answers - Sheets 1 to 18

1
(in any order) **Numbers less than 10**: three, four, five, six, seven, nine
(in any order) **Numbers more than 10**: thirteen, fourteen, fifteen, sixteen, seventeen, nineteen

2
1. more **2.** sum **3.** equals **4.** double **5.** altogether **6.** difference **7.** make

3
19 - nineteen, 90 - ninety, 100 - one hundred, 800 - eight hundred, 1000 - one thousand
first, third, fifth, sixth, seventh, ninth, last

4
PENNY, BUY, SELL, SPEND, CHANGE, CHEAP, PRICE, COIN
The letters of each word on the wordsearch should be connected by a coloured line.

5
1. correct **2.** second **3.** wrong **4.** predict **5.** pound **6.** nearly **7.** fraction **8.** once

6
1. ADDITION **2.** DIGIT **3.** THIRD **4.** SYMBOL **5.** EIGHTY **6.** EVEN **7.** ELEVENTH **8.** TENTH
9. CONTINUE **10.** RIGHT

7
1. sold **2.** roughly **3.** cheaper **4.** label **5.** less **6.** pence **7.** pay **8.** Most

8
1. before **2.** dear **3.** first **4.** guess **5.** exact **6.** group **7.** exchange **8.** array

9
Across: **1.** ANSWER **5.** TWO **6.** ROUND **7.** THIN **9.** INTO
Down: **1.** AFTER **2.** SCORE **3.** ENOUGH **4.** ODD **7.** TO **8.** NO

10
(in any order) **Numbers less than 60**: twenty-one, thirty-six, thirty-eight, forty-two, fifty-three,
fifty-nine   (in any order) **Numbers more than 60**: sixty-three, sixty-eight, seventy-seven,
eighty-two, eighty-nine, ninety-five

11
1. divide **2.** multiply **3.** column **4.** divided **5.** row **6.** multiplied **7.** halve

12
Row 1 - whole, three-quarters, quarter, half   **Row 2 -** three-quarters, quarter, half, whole
Row 3 - whole, half, three-quarters, quarter

13
add, divide, times, plus, share, multiply, minus, subtract
The letters of each word on the wordsearch should be connected by a coloured line.

14
1. twice **2.** total **3.** pair **4.** cost **5.** last **6.** fourth **7.** fifty **8.** estimate

15
1. calculate **2.** least **3.** title **4.** table **5.** tally **6.** vote **7.** compare **8.** between **9.** next **10.** bought

16
1. set **2.** count **3.** pictogram **4.** list **5.** graph **6.** table **7.** Tally

17
1. morning **2.** holiday **3.** middle **4.** bend **5.** month **6.** clock **7.** behind **8.** fortnight

18
Across: **1.** heavy **4.** grams **5.** light **6.** weeks **8.** edge
Down: **1.** high **2.** analogue **3.** yes **5.** low **7.** end

Answers - Sheets 19 to 36

19	(in any order) **2D shapes**: square, star, circle, rectangle, pentagon, triangle (in any order) **3D shapes**: cone, cube, cylinder, pyramid, cuboid, sphere
20	**1.** compare **2.** lighter **3.** metre **4.** width **5.** ruler **6.** narrow **7.** height
21	**1.** CURVED **2.** SOMETIMES **3.** POINT **4.** QUICKEST **5.** SHORTER **6.** SLOWER **7.** CONTAINS
22	HEAVY, LIGHT, SCALES, WEIGHT, LENGTH, BALANCE, KILOGRAM, CENTIMETRE The letters of each word on the wordsearch should be connected by a coloured line.
23	**1.** winter **2.** below **3.** watch **4.** autumn **5.** centre **6.** summer **7.** year **8.** spring
24	**1.** TOMORROW **2.** OLDER **3.** DIGITAL **4.** BEDTIME **5.** SIDE **6.** HOLLOW **7.** ACROSS **8.** LATE **9.** SLOWEST **10.** NEWEST
25	**1.** clockwise **2.** back **3.** higher **4.** forwards **5.** journey, apart **6.** top **7.** under
26	**1.** night **2.** never **3.** sideways **4.** position **5.** quick **6.** octagon **7.** round **8.** outside
27	**Across**: **1.** LONG **4.** TOWARDS **6.** NOW **9.** ON **10.** TIME **Down**: **1.** LITRE **2.** NEW **3.** WIDE **5.** ABOUT **7.** ONE **8.** IN
28	**1.** January **2.** February **3.** March **4.** April **5.** May **6.** June **7.** July **8.** August **9.** September **10.** October **11.** November **12.** December.
29	**1.** size **2.** further **3.** far **4.** close **5.** lightest **6.** shallow, depth **7.** Deep
30	**1.** WEEKEND **2.** MONDAY **3.** REFLECTION **4.** TRIANGULAR **5.** TALLEST **6.** APART **7.** FRIDAY **8.** HANDS
31	full, above, slow, hold, empty, capacity, millilitre, container The letters of each word on the wordsearch should be connected by a coloured line.
32	**1.** drawing **2.** oldest **3.** Thursday **4.** hexagon **5.** midnight **6.** minutes **7.** near **8.** flat
33	**1.** birthday **2.** inside **3.** always **4.** fold **5.** today **6.** deep **7.** evening **8.** beside **9.** opposite **10.** through
34	**1.** up **2.** backwards **3.** lower **4.** clockwise **5.** sideways **6.** front **7.** bottom **8.** over
35	**1.** soon **2.** slide **3.** Saturday **4.** solid **5.** route **6.** second **7.** thick **8.** straight
36	**Across**: **1.** shape **3.** often **4.** three **6.** hour **7.** money **Down**: **1.** short **2.** afternoon **5.** early **8.** on

Maths Vocabulary CHALLENGE

How Well Have I Done? - Individual Record Sheet

Name _____ Class _____

Sheet	Date	Comments	Mark	Poss Mark		Sheet	Date	Comments	Mark	Poss Mark
1				12		19				12
2				7		20				7
3				10		21				7
4				8		22				8
5				8		23				8
6				10		24				10
7				8		25				8
8				8		26				8
9				11		27				11
10				12		28				12
11				7		29				8
12				12		30				8
13				8		31				8
14				8		32				8
15				10		33				10
16				7		34				8
17				8		35				8
18				10		36				9

Sixteen Spelling Tests

Number and handling data

(easier words)	(harder words)
1. add	1. exchange
2. count	2. calculate
3. first	3. bought
4. price	4. altogether
5. third	5. thousand
6. spend	6. difference
7. coin	7. compare
8. double	8. guess
9. total	9. continue
10. divide	10. pictogram

(easier words)	(harder words)
1. buy	1. multiply
2. pence	2. fraction
3. share	3. enough
4. even	4. estimate
5. last	5. least
6. once	6. calculation
7. before	7. exact
8. times	8. symbol
9. digit	9. hundred
10. minus	10. predict

(easier words)	(harder words)
1. odd	1. pattern
2. plus	2. quarter
3. equals	3. graph
4. twice	4. roughly
5. cost	5. subtract
6. half	6. column
7. answer	7. addition
8. round	8. between
9. row	9. eleventh
10. tally	10. multiplied

(easier words)	(harder words)
1. sell	1. array
2. after	2. seventh
3. wrong	3. exactly
4. cheap	4. thirteen
5. fifty	5. represent
6. right	6. divided
7. vote	7. operation
8. list	8. seventeen
9. title	9. thirty-eight
10. penny	10. sequence

Shape, space and measures

(easier words)	(harder words)
1. back	1. birthday
2. flat	2. length
3. hour	3. further
4. under	4. pyramid
5. apart	5. September
6. wide	6. centimetre
7. cone	7. triangular
8. round	8. balance
9. edge	9. Thursday
10. metre	10. octagon

(easier words)	(harder words)
1. bend	1. height
2. older	2. centre
3. gram	3. kilogram
4. year	4. triangle
5. fold	5. afternoon
6. hollow	6. pentagon
7. about	7. container
8. month	8. August
9. deep	9. sometimes
10. front	10. direction

(easier words)	(harder words)
1. clock	1. fortnight
2. narrow	2. backwards
3. ruler	3. measure
4. corner	4. sphere
5. early	5. position
6. high	6. capacity
7. circle	7. weight
8. late	8. analogue
9. middle	9. rectangle
10. behind	10. January

(easier words)	(harder words)
1. end	1. digital
2. often	2. opposite
3. cube	3. tomorrow
4. litre	4. autumn
5. below	5. hexagon
6. roll	6. clockwise
7. close	7. February
8. full	8. cylinder
9. across	9. straight
10. empty	10. millilitre